OCEANS ALIVE

Parrotfish

by Martha E. H. Rustad

BELLWETHER MEDIA · MINNEAPOLIS, MN

Note to Librarians, Teachers, and Parents:

Blastoff! Readers are carefully developed by literacy experts and combine standards-based content with developmentally-appropriate text.

Level 1 provides the most support through repetition of high-frequency words, light text, predictable sentence patterns, and strong visual support.

Level 2 offers early readers a bit more challenge through varied simple sentences, increased text load, and less repetition of high frequency words.

Level 3 advances early-fluent readers toward fluency through increased text and concept load, less reliance on visuals, longer sentences, and more literary language.

Level 4 builds reading stamina by providing more text per page, increased use of punctuation, greater variation in sentence patterns, and increasingly challenging vocabulary.

Level 5 encourages children to move from "learning to read" to "reading to learn" by providing even more text, varied writing styles, and less familiar topics.

Whichever book is right for your reader, Blastoff! Readers are the perfect books to build confidence and encourage a love of reading that will last a lifetime!

This edition first published in 2008 by Bellwether Media.

No part of this publication may be reproduced in whole or in part without written permission of the publisher. For information regarding permission, write to Bellwether Media Inc., Attention: Permissions Department, Post Office Box 1C, Minnetonka, MN 55345-9998.

Library of Congress Cataloging-in-Publication Data
Rustad, Martha E. H. (Martha Elizabeth Hillman), 1975–
  Parrotfish / by Martha E.H. Rustad.
    p. cm. — (Blastoff! readers. Oceans alive)
Summary: "Simple text and supportive images introduce beginning readers to parrotfish. Intended for students in kindergarten through third grade"—Provided by publisher.
  Includes bibliographical references and index.
  ISBN-13: 978-1-60014-079-2 (hardcover : alk. paper)
  ISBN-10: 1-60014-079-3 (hardcover : alk. paper)
  1. Parrotfishes—Juvenile literature. I. Title.

  QL638.S3R87 2008
  597'.7–dc22   2007009796

Contents

Parrotfish are colorful fish.
They swim in shallow
ocean water.

4

Some parrotfish are small.
Other parrotfish can grow
as big as you!

Thick **scales** cover a parrotfish's body. Each scale can be a different color.

6

Parrotfish change colors as
they grow.

Many parrotfish swim
in groups called **schools**.

8

Parrotfish use their side **fins** to swim forward. Most other fish use their tail fin.

Parrotfish have teeth that are stuck together. The teeth look like a parrot's beak.

10

Their teeth never stop growing.

Parrotfish eat small living things called **algae**. Algae live inside **coral**.

Coral is the **skeleton** of a small ocean animal. Corals pile up and become **coral reefs.**

Parrotfish bite off chunks of coral to get algae.

14

Biting hard coral helps parrotfish wear down their teeth.

Parrotfish crush and eat coral with their teeth. Their bodies turn it into white coral sand.

Parrotfish drop the sand out of their bodies onto the ocean floor.

Parrotfish rest at night.
Sometimes they make
slime to cover their bodies.

18

Sharks, eels, and other **predators** cannot smell them through the slime.

Parrotfish rest safely in the slime until morning.

Then they start another
busy day eating algae
and dropping sand.

21

Glossary

algae—tiny living things that grow in water

coral—a tiny ocean animal with a small skeleton

coral reef—a structure in the ocean made of the skeletons of many corals

fins—flaps on a fish's body used for moving and steering through water

predator—an animal that hunts other animals for food

scales—hard plates that cover the body of a fish

school—a group of fish

skeleton—a hard structure that supports and protects the body of an animal

slime—a clear liquid that covers the body of a parrotfish

To Learn More

AT THE LIBRARY

Cole, Melissa. *Coral Reefs*. Farmington Hills, Mich.: Blackbirch Press, 2004.

Giles, Bridget. *Parrotfish*. Danbury, Conn.: Grolier Educational, 2001.

Rake, Jody Sullivan. *Parrotfish*. Mankato, Minn.: Capstone Press, 2006.

Whitehouse, Patricia. *Hiding in a Coral Reef*. Chicago, Ill.: Heinemann Library, 2003.

ON THE WEB

Learning more about parrotfish is as easy as 1, 2, 3.

1. Go to www.factsurfer.com

2. Enter "parrotfish" into search box.

3. Click the "Surf" button and you will see a list of related web sites.

With factsurfer.com, finding more information is just a click away.

Index

The photographs in this book are reproduced through the courtesy of: Jeff Hunter/Getty Images, front cover, pp. 7, 10, 20-21; Hemis/Alamy, pp. 4-5; Chris A. Crumley/Alamy, p. 6; Images and Stories/Alamy, pp. 8-9; Reinhard Dirscherl/Alamy, p. 11; Georgie Holland/Age fotostock, pp. 12-13, 14-15; Wolfgang Amri, p. 16; Paul Sutherland/Getty Images, p. 17; Mike Severns/Getty Images, pp. 18-19.